Is There Anybody There?

A Play

Lee Flewitt

A SAMUEL FRENCH ACTING EDITION

SAMUEL FRENCH

FOUNDED 1830

SAMUELFRENCH-LONDON.CO.UK
SAMUELFRENCH.COM

FOR AMATEUR PRODUCTION ENQUIRIES

UNITED KINGDOM AND WORLD
EXCLUDING NORTH AMERICA
plays@SamuelFrench-London.co.uk
020 7255 4302/01

Each title is subject to availability from Samuel French,

depending upon country of performance.

IS THERE ANYBODY THERE?

First performed by the Alderney Theatre Group on 5th August, 1997, at the Island Hall, Alderney, Channel Islands:

Mrs Carrington	Andre Gaydon
Mary	Alex Harrison
Hopkins	Tim Butler
Lady Gilbert	Barbara Featherstone
Lord Gilbert	Bill Walden
Dr Wilson	Robin Whicker
Miss Reid	Candy Osborne
Patterson	Philip Hatcher

The play was directed by **Charlotte Matimong**

ASM Wendy Hamon

CHARACTERS

Mrs Carrington, middle-aged
Mary, young
Hopkins, young
Lady Gilbert, middle-aged
Lord Gilbert, middle-aged
Dr Wilson, middle-aged
Miss Reid, young
Patterson, young

The action of the play takes place in Mrs Carrington's parlour in the Whitechapel area of London

Period: late Victorian

IS THERE ANYBODY THERE?

Mrs Carrington's parlour in the Whitechapel area of London

There is a table, six chairs, a couch, a side table and a rocking chair nearby. The table holds a crystal ball. On the side table is a drinks tray with a pitcher of water, a bottle of brandy, and glasses. There are bookshelves holding books and a vase. Gas lamps, pictures, a mirror and a clock are on the wall

The Curtain *opens to reveal Mrs Carrington sitting alone at the table in the dark, facing the audience with her head bowed. The crystal ball glows in front of her. The clock ticks loudly, then chimes thirteen times at which point Mrs Carrington inhales deeply and raises her head.*

Mrs Carrington Is there anybody there? (*She pauses. More emphatically*) Is there anybody there?

The crystal ball and the gas lamps on the wall flicker slightly. Mrs Carrington shudders as if with a chill

Aaaahh. Somebody is there. I can feel the cold draught of the grave. Enter, spirit, you are among friends.

The door slowly opens and closes on squeaky hinges. We hear footsteps cross the room

Be seated spirit, and let us know your name.

The rocking chair starts to rock

Why, it is my old friend, Chief Red Cloud of the Apache tribe. Have you come to intercede for us tonight? (*She listens for a moment, nodding, then breaks the trance to address an unseen audience*) I thought so. He has brought another with him. One who has recently departed this life. A soul in great torment and confusion. As with all sudden death, its occurrence brought certain ... inconveniences. There was unfinished business, and this has made the spirit restless. Some of them just can't let go, you see, if they feel there is a matter left … unresolved. (*She cocks her head and listens for a moment*) I understand. Is there one among us who used to be known as Beaky? I am sure I know no-one of that name, but perhaps… (*She stops, as if interrupted by an invisible guest at her side*) Did you say something, Lady Fanshawe? (*She pauses*) You were known as Beaky in your childhood. Not in reference to that enormous nose of yours, I hope. Then our revenant guest must mean you. I shall ask him, dear. (*She enters the trance again*) Restless spirit, identify yourself. (*She pauses*) Wicks, is it? Wickens? Wickson! Wickson, the gardener's boy, who fell from the apple tree last month and broke his back. How he sorrows! (*She listens again, muttering*) Oh, you poor little fellow, how awful! (*She breaks out of her trance and addresses her "guest"*) It would seem, your ladyship, that the poor boy suffered a terror of heights, yet, despite this there were ripe apples to be plucked from the topmost branches of the tree, which you simply couldn't wait for. And now his parents are childless, their future uncertain, and this has angered young Wickson. He cannot rest until he is sure that they are recompensed for their loss. (*She pauses*) I can feel his anger, so vengeful. It must find expression!

Books fly off the bookshelves, a picture is dislodged from the wall, a vase breaks and general havoc ensues with a storm of sound effects. The table rises from the floor, hovering

Mrs Carrington leaps to her feet, hands aloft

Spirits, cease!

And all becomes abruptly still, except for the table, which continues to hover. Mrs Carrington puts a hand on it and tuts

Spirits cease, Mr Hopkins!

The table drops with a clatter. Mrs Carrington sighs, returns to her trance

I fear the child will not be at peace, my lady, until he feels some compensation has been made to his grieving parents. On the subject of compensation, I am sure I heard the sound of breaking porcelain. The vase, you say. A trifling matter. I will add the cost to your account. That particular dynasty is still quite obtainable. Please don't bother with the mess. I employ a worthless little skivvy for that chore.

The Lights come up

Mary enters, beaming

What do you think, Mary?

Mary If that doesn't rattle the old duchess, ma'am, nothing will. I thought the vase was a nice touch. Let's hope they don't want to examine the evidence.

Mrs Carrington Gentlefolk don't stoop to such things, Mary. Her ladyship would much rather pay than demean herself.

Mary Not when it comes to my Uncle Percy and his missis, she wouldn't, ma'am. Their little Tommy dead because of her neglect, and barely a kind word spoke about it.

Mrs Carrington I'm sure their fortunes will improve after her ladyship's appointment tomorrow night, my dear.

Mary Thanks to you, ma'am. I do appreciate it. I wouldn't have asked in the first place, but Uncle Percy was so distraught. I knew you would think of something.

Mrs Carrington It's no trouble, Mary. I quite relish the prospect of fleecing the old skinflint for a noble cause. Now then. Where did I leave my cane?

Mary Here it is, ma'am. (*She hands Mrs Carrington a white cane*) Sit yourself down while I tidy up the place.

Mrs Carrington You had better summon Mr Hopkins while you're about it.

Mary Yes, ma'am.

Mary pulls back a rug and exposes a trap door. (See Notes p. 30 for this effect) She lifts it while Mrs Carrington continues

Mrs Carrington If we are to pull this off smoothly, this table has to rise slowly from the floor and fall gently on cue. Not hop around like some skittish thoroughbred.

Mary (*shouting*) You can come up now, Hopkins. Mrs Carrington would like a word with you.

Hopkins enters. He appears in profile so that the scarred side of his face is hidden, for the moment, from the audience

You've been a naughty boy.

Hopkins glares at her. Mary straightens pictures and picks up books, pottery, etc.

Hopkins Is something the matter, ma'am?

Mrs Carrington How long have you been with us now, Mr Hopkins?

Hopkins This will be my third week, ma'am.

Mrs Carrington And do you enjoy the work? I trust it isn't too demanding?

Hopkins Yes, ma'am—I mean, no, ma'am.

Mrs Carrington Then I suggest, if you wish to extend your tenure into a fourth week, that you learn your cues.

Hopkins You mean the table, ma'am.

Mrs Carrington Precisely. Before your predecessor, Mr Hancock, began his enforced sojourn to Her Majesty's colonies in Australia, he spoke very highly of you. Apparently you shared accommodation in Shepherd's Bush at one time?

Hopkins Yes, ma'am. The Scrubs.

Mrs Carrington (*surprised a little*) I see. Well; if you had only absorbed an ounce of Mr Hancock's immaculate timing…

Hopkins It's the floor, ma'am. Solid oak, it is. And what with all the rollers and pulleys clanging, I can barely hear a thing. And then the table mechanism jammed…

Mary Leaping about like a thorough-skittish-bred, it was. Quite unseemly.

Mrs Carrington Thank you, Mary. You realize, do you not, Mr Hopkins, that if any doubt were to be cast on my reputation as a clairvoyant, there would be no more easy life for any of us.

Hopkins Yes, ma'am.

Mrs Carrington My guests will be sitting around the table. It must rise smoothly and hover for a minute or so, and then resume its original place.

Hopkins Yes, ma'am. I'll see that it does.

Mrs Carrington Are you all right down there? It's not too dark?

Hopkins No, ma'am. I'm quite at home in the dark.

Mary (*sotto voce*) No blooming wonder.

Mrs Carrington And are you receiving the cues from Mary?

Hopkins When she sends them, ma'am.

Mrs Carrington And are you sending them, Mary?

Mary (*glaring at Hopkins*) Yes, ma'am. As soon as I hear you say, "It must find expression", I push the switch to alert Mr H, and then start shoving the books through the backs of the shelves. As soon as you say "Spirits cease", I push the switch again and he lowers the table.

Mrs Carrington Or not, as the case may be.

Hopkins Ma'am.

Mrs Carrington Let's run through it together. First cue…

Mary "Is there anybody there?" I adjust the gas supply to the lamps from outside the room.

Mrs Carrington Not so bright next time, Mary. Let's try to keep them in the dark for as long as possible.

Mary Yes, ma'am. Though how you can tell, beats me.

Mrs Carrington I have ears, Mary. There is a quite audible hiss when the lamps are turned up. Next cue…

Mary "You are among friends." I open and close the door. (*She looks at Hopkins pointedly*)

Hopkins Oh. I walk across the ceiling in the cellar and work the rocking chair.

Mrs Carrington Not until I say, "Be seated". Although it did occur to me that if Chief Red Cloud is an American Indian, he would hardly be wearing hob-nailed boots.

Hopkins Indeed, ma'am. But the effect might be lost using moccasins.

Mrs Carrington Good point.

Mary Maybe you could swap your Indian guide for a Regimental Sergeant Major, ma'am.

Mrs Carrington Do I hear the kettle, Mary?

Mary exits in a huff

Hopkins smiles to himself

Come and sit down, Mr Hopkins, and let's go over your report. Miss Reid first. How has she filled her time since her last visit to me?

Hopkins She seems in remarkably high spirits, ma'am, considering her recent loss.

Mrs Carrington Her mother, yes. I would hazard that the demise of Mrs Reid senior was less of a blow to dear Elizabeth than she gave us to believe. You recall how the old woman used to bully the poor girl when they came here.

Hopkins A bit of a dragon, ma'am. She's better off without her, in my opinion.

Mrs Carrington Quite. Please continue.

Hopkins Miss Reid has had the house decorated throughout, ma'am. I don't think her mother would have approved of the colour.

Mrs Carrington Let me guess: pink.

Hopkins Everywhere, ma'am. While she was out to church on Sunday, I stole into the house and had a swift look around.

Mrs Carrington You were careful to cover your tracks, I hope. She mustn't suspect that the house has been entered in her absence. That would spoil everything.

Hopkins Yes, ma'am.

Mrs Carrington Did you conceal anything for me?

Hopkins A gold charm bracelet, ma'am. I placed it under the rug in her dressing room. It should be found quite easily.

Mrs Carrington Good. I don't suppose it's a subtle shade of pink.
Hopkins Not really, ma'am. It might be described as puce.
Mrs Carrington It sounds quite horrendous. I often think it's almost a blessing to have gone blind, Mr Hopkins. One is spared so much ugliness.

Hopkins says nothing, but bows his head. There is a brief, uncomfortable pause

What else did you learn?
Hopkins Her canary died, ma'am. She had him in a shoe box which I found in the conservatory.
Mrs Carrington Her mother's canary, Mr Hopkins. The last link with her former life. Did you, perchance, examine the little fellow?
Hopkins Why, no, ma'am. Why should I?
Mrs Carrington No reason in particular. Yellow and pink... Do go on.
Hopkins There have been more letters from Captain Patterson.
Mrs Carrington That same fellow she brought with her a fortnight ago. It didn't take him long. Offers of marriage, I suppose.
Hopkins That and other things, ma'am. He's a smooth one, right enough.
Mrs Carrington Too smooth, if you ask me, Hopkins. Miss Elizabeth Reid and her newly acquired inheritance would be quite a prize for the likes of the penniless Captain. He might be a threat to us.
Hopkins How so, ma'am?
Mrs Carrington His manner at our last meeting was quite overtly cynical. He could win Miss Reid away, and that wouldn't do at all. Gullible spinsters are at a premium in this profession. Especially those with money.
Hopkins I wouldn't worry too much about it, Mrs Carrington. She hasn't exactly snapped him up, has she?
Mrs Carrington That's all part of the courting ritual, Mr Hopkins. There are certain proprieties to be observed, one of which is the early display of a seeming indifference to the would-be suitor. The signs are all there.
Hopkins I wouldn't know about such things, ma'am.
Mrs Carrington No? You mean, there's no special lady in your life? Surely not, Mr Hopkins.
Hopkins Well. It's hard to say really. I mean, there is somebody...

He looks at her meaningfully, extends a hand to hers, but snatches it away as Mary enters

Mary You are a tease, ma'am. I hadn't even put the kettle on.
Mrs Carrington Forgive me, my dear. In your absence, Mr Hopkins and I were discussing Miss Reid and Captain Patterson.

Mary He's a chancer, that one. He put his hands on my waist on his last visit. Made it look like an accident, but I know a squeeze when I feel one.
Hopkins I'll wager you do.

Mary sneers at him

Mrs Carrington Let's get on, shall we? What of the dashing Captain's movements, Mr Hopkins?
Hopkins Much as we thought, ma'am: He pays court to Miss Reid during the day and indulges his other … interests in the evenings. I followed him to the *Pig and Whistle* in Whitechapel on Tuesday night, where he fell in with—how shall I put it—low company.
Mary Scandalous!
Mrs Carrington Of the female persuasion, I assume.
Hopkins Yes, ma'am. I saw money change hands and followed him and his consort as far as decency allowed. He returned to the pub about half an hour later with the woman, and they drank together until she was engaged by another gentleman. He returned to Chelsea barracks at about eleven o'clock.
Mary That poor Miss Reid. If she but knew what a bounder he is.
Mrs Carrington It would certainly put paid to his ambitions of marriage to the lady. And might serve our own interests too … we shall see. You have done well, Mr Hopkins, and I apologise if I was a little harsh with you earlier.
Hopkins Thank you, ma'am.
Mary He'd better get that table fixed. Your guests will be here before long.
Mrs Carrington Oh, yes. Mr Hopkins?
Hopkins I'll see to it right away, ma'am.
Mary Back into your little hole, then.

Hopkins and Mary exchange looks of mutual dislike as he descends through the trap

When he has disappeared, Mary roughly kicks the trap door closed. Mrs Carrington jumps

Sorry, ma'am. I dropped it.
Mrs Carrington I do wish you would try to get on with Hopkins, Mary. He really isn't so bad.
Mary Face like a gargoyle and a temper to match. I can't abide the sight of him.
Mrs Carrington Can't abide the sight of him? That's a little bit strong, he seems civil enough to me.

Mary That's 'cos *you're* the only person I've ever seen him be civil to. Thank God he doesn't live in.

Mrs Carrington I must admit, Mr Hancock's company was a little more diverting. I miss him.

Mary (*wistfully*) He was a rogue, ma'am. But a lovable one.

Mrs Carrington Still. As long as I have you, dear Mary. Sit by me and tell me what you know about the Gilberts. Just the relevant high points, if you please.

Mary withdraws her notebook from the pocket of her apron

Mary On Saturday, I followed Lord and Lady Gilbert to a piano recital at the home of Sir Rupert Montgomery in Belgravia. They left early at 9 p.m. I heard her ladyship complaining of a headache as they got into their carriage. On Sunday, they went to church. The sermon was on the sanctity of all life. Sang *All Things Bright and Beautiful* and *Nearer My God To Thee*. Monday, Lady Gilbert bought a new hat with a stuffed bird in it— revolting old thing——

Mrs Carrington The hat or the bird, dear?

Mary Her ladyship, ma'am. Sheer hypocrisy, is what I call it.

Mrs Carrington Oh, Mary. You are a treasure. If everybody was as astute as you I would have no custom at all. Now tell me about this friend of theirs, this Dr Wilson? Is it the same man whose name is so often in the newspapers?

Mary Yes, ma'am. The doctor is, according to a press statement— "overseeing a new project among the capital's needy".

Mrs Carrington And you found out what this project is, of course.

Mary A charitable hospital, ma'am. Quite nearby as it happens. Dr Wilson has taken a room on the premises so that he can be in constant attendance.

Mrs Carrington How noble of him. But I fear he is wasting his time there.

Mary How so, ma'am?

Mrs Carrington The poor will not be helped, Mary. In fact, it is vital that they are not, for they are part of a larger, finely balanced system which we tamper with at our peril. Look at France, with their revolutions. Clueless anarchists running about like headless chickens.

Mary But how can making sick people better be a bad thing?

Mrs Carrington You don't understand, Mary. If you improve the physical health alone of the poor, they will merely return the kindness by procreating more of their own, thereby worsening their lot in the long run. There will be less to go around, which means more suffering and death. By which tragic means the balance is achieved again.

Mary I think I understand. But I'm not sure it applies in the good doctor's case.

Mrs Carrington Explain.

Mary Well, he's not really keeping folk from death's door, so to speak. It's a particular kind of suffering which he is concerned with. (*She falters uncertainly, unwilling to say any more*)

Mrs Carrington Mary?

Mary Ma'am?

Mrs Carrington You can't leave it there, my dear. What is it that he does?

Mary (*struggling*) It's eyes, ma'am.

Mrs Carrington (*after a brief moment of comprehension*) Ah.

Mary Doctor Wilson's chief interest appears to be among the blind and partially sighted. The poor, it seems, are especially prone to those diseases which cause it.

Mrs Carrington I see. Or, rather … never mind. So, the good doctor is a man of many parts: medic *and* social reformer. It will be quite a challenge to make a believer out of him.

Mary What makes you think he isn't a believer already?

Mrs Carrington My dear girl, by the very nature of his profession, and his experiences with the criminal fraternity, Dr Wilson is bound to be more sceptical than our usual clientele. If that were not the case, I believe that her ladyship would not have invited him to this evening's meeting.

Mary You mean, her ladyship doesn't believe either.

Mrs Carrington I mean, like everybody else, she has doubts. She feels the need to test her faith, and Dr Wilson is to be the instrument of that test. Which is why we must be especially convincing tonight. They will be here very soon. Is the room tidied, Mary?

Mary Yes, ma'am.

Mrs Carrington You had better signal Mr Hopkins to be ready, then.

Mary Right you are, ma'am.

Mary exits

Mrs Carrington sits and picks up a book. The illusion of time passing should be conveyed by the ticking of the clock. After a period of about fifteen seconds, we hear, off stage, the sound of knocking at the front door and voices from outside the room. Mrs Carrington rises and prepares to receive her guests

Lady Gilbert (*off*) Good evening, Mary.

Mary (*off*) Good evening, ma'am. Lord Gilbert. Let me take your coats. Good evening, Sir.

Dr Wilson (*off*) Good evening.

Mary knocks and enters the room

Mary Your guests have arrived, ma'am.
Mrs Carrington Show them in, Mary.

Mary exits

Lady Gilbert enters first, followed by Lord Gilbert and Dr Wilson

Lady Gilbert Mrs Carrington, how lovely to see you again.
Mrs Carrington Lady Gilbert. Gentlemen.
Lady Gilbert We came directly by hansom and instructed the driver to return promptly at 10 o'clock. There's been another one, you know?
Mrs Carrington Another one? I'm sorry...
Lord Gilbert Another murder! That's three so far.
Lady Gilbert Last night. Some poor woman cut to pieces in Whitechapel. They say it's quite inhuman what he does to them.
Dr Wilson Don't fret yourself, Cynthia. You'll have another turn.
Mrs Carrington Another turn?
Lady Gilbert I had a dizzy spell on the doorstep. It's this area. How can you live here? So close to his ... his hunting ground.

Lady Gilbert sits, comforted by Lord Gilbert

Lord Gilbert There now, dear. Don't worry yourself. He doesn't go after people like us.
Dr Wilson Allow me to introduce myself. Dr John Wilson.

Mrs Carrington shakes hands with him

Mrs Carrington I am familiar with your work, Doctor. At least, I have read accounts of your exploits, in the newspapers.
Dr Wilson Lord and Lady Gilbert have told me a great deal about you, madam. I also believe we have another mutual acquaintance.
Mrs Carrington I'm not sure...
Lady Gilbert John is my own aunt's godson, dear. We found each other again at her funeral last year. Imagine my surprise when I discovered that the boy I had known in my youth was the eminent Dr Wilson.
Mrs Carrington I'm taken aback. It hasn't been mentioned at all.
Lord Gilbert It must have slipped the old lady's mind. So many things did in her latter days.
Dr Wilson The dead are notoriously reticent, I always find.
Mrs Carrington (*light-heartedly*) I sense an unbeliever in our midst! I do hope you have brought an open mind with you, Doctor.

Lady Gilbert John has seen far stranger things than those which occur in this room, my dear.
Dr Wilson Yes. And I usually get to the truth of them.

Knocking and more voices off

Miss Reid (*off*) Good evening, Mary.
Mary (*off*) Good evening, Miss Reid. Captain Patterson, may I take your coats?
Mrs Carrington (*relieved*) I believe our other guests have arrived.

A knock on the door

Mary enters with Captain Patterson and Miss Reid

Mary Captain Patterson and Miss Reid, ma'am.
Mrs Carrington Thank you, Mary. Bring us some tea, would you?
Mary Yes, ma'am.
Mrs Carrington And perhaps something a little stronger for Lady Gilbert? For your nerves, dear.
Lady Gilbert Thank you, no. I've never allowed strong spirits to enter my body.
Patterson That's Mrs Carrington's job, surely. What?
Miss Reid That will do, Edward. Don't take any notice of him, Mrs Carrington.
Mrs Carrington Just the tea then, Mary.
Mary Right away, ma'am.

Mary exits

Mrs Carrington So, we are all here. Good. Dr Wilson, may I introduce you to Miss Reid and Captain Patterson.

Dr Wilson bows to Miss Reid and shakes Patterson's hand

Dr Wilson I've heard so much about you, I feel as if I've met you all before.
Miss Reid How very strange. Edward and I had a very similar experience in the street just now.
Patterson Don't bother them with that silly thing.
Lady Gilbert Oh, but please do.
Mrs Carrington Yes. Do go on.
Miss Reid Well, it was quite unsettling really. As Edward and I were approaching your front door, we were apprehended by a young girl.

Patterson Hardly a girl. A woman really.

Miss Reid Sixteen or so, I would think. It's difficult to say when they're so grubby.

Dr Wilson But you recognized her?

Miss Reid No. Quite the opposite. She seemed to think she knew us. Or Edward, at least.

Lady Gilbert Good Lord!

Miss Reid Yes. Called him Teddy, of all things. Asked him for some money and then said something unutterably vulgar to me.

Mrs Carrington What did you do?

Miss Reid Edward gave her a few pennies and a jolly stern talking to. Took her to one side to protect my sensibilities.

Dr Wilson I see.

Patterson Do you?

Lord Gilbert You obviously resemble someone she knows.

Miss Reid And the same name also. Isn't it too uncanny?

Lady Gilbert I hope you gave her enough for a cab fare. No woman should have to walk these streets after dark.

Miss Reid It should be all right. It is Friday.

Mrs Carrington What's that got to do with anything?

Dr Wilson The murderer has always struck on a Thursday night. Three weeks—three Thursdays—three murdered women.

Patterson Prostitutes.

Miss Reid Edward!

Dr Wilson It's true. All the victims have been loose women working in the district of Whitechapel, not too far from here. All horribly mutilated in a frenzied attack.

Lady Gilbert You mustn't go to your Club on Thursday any more, Bernard. I can't be alone in the house with such a monster on the loose.

Lord Gilbert The house is full of servants, dear.

Lady Gilbert It's not the same.

Mrs Carrington You seem very knowledgeable, Doctor.

Dr Wilson Yes. The police have asked me to assist in their investigation.

Patterson Indeed. So, what is the latest news?

Dr Wilson I really can't say. I render technical assistance only. The investigation is sealed closed from any outsiders.

Mrs Carrington What kind of technical assistance?

Dr Wilson Again, I can't say.

Mrs Carrington Can't or won't say?

Dr Wilson smiles

Miss Reid Perhaps it's better *not* to know some things.

Patterson What are you thinking about? If the Doctor knows something, surely we should know about it. For our own protection, at least.

Lady Gilbert Is it the Ripper, John? Is that what you aren't allowed to tell us?

Patterson He is hardly likely to say, is he?

Dr Wilson It isn't the Ripper, Cynthia. Of that we are almost certain.

Mrs Carrington *Modus operandi.* Isn't that what you call it?

Dr Wilson Yes. These killers have a particular method of operating—a signature, if you like—which makes one quite distinct from another.

Lord Gilbert And this killer's signature is that distinct?

Dr Wilson Oh yes. Unique, in fact.

Patterson Oh, come on, Doctor. Don't be a tease.

Mrs Carrington I believe the Doctor has very good reasons for witholding his information, Captain Patterson.

Patterson And what might they be? He's certainly getting the lion's share of our attention.

Dr Wilson I can assure you, Captain Patterson, that I have the best possible reasons. In cases like this one, so many people come forward—foolish or mentally unstable people—claiming to be the perpetrator of the crimes.

Mrs Carrington And so you keep something back. Something only the real killer would know.

Dr Wilson Precisely. And that is why I can say no more on the subject.

Mrs Carrington What is keeping Mary with the tea?

Miss Reid Can't we just get on? I have no real desire to be out of doors tonight.

Lady Gilbert I agree. We didn't come here to discuss this fiend in Whitechapel. Help me up, Bernard.

Mrs Carrington I don't like to start before Mary comes back. She will have to interrupt us. It might disturb the spirits.

Lady Gilbert But we always start at this time. Mary should realize that.

They all begin to take their seats around the table

Miss Reid Would you sit beside me, Doctor? I feel so much safer with a medical man beside me.

Patterson scowls

Mrs Carrington I'm still not sure. If Mary should come in…

Lord Gilbert She will immediately see the seance is in session and proceed with caution. I am turning down the gas lamps. (*He does so*)

Lady Gilbert Please sit down, Mrs Carrington.

*Lord Gilbert and Mrs Carrington take their places. Everyone holds hands.
Patterson scowls at Miss Reid and Dr Wilson holding hands, across the table*

Mrs Carrington Very well. I will do what I can. (*She takes a deep breath*)
   Is there anybody there?

A pause

   Is there anybody there?

Nothing happens. Mrs Carrington shakes her head

   I'm sorry. I really don't think it's going to work.
Lady Gilbert Keep trying, dear. We don't want to disappoint the doctor, do
   we?
Mrs Carrington It's not entirely up to me——

The clock begins to chime and Mrs Carrington smiles to herself

   (*Sotto voce*) Good girl, Mary.

The clock stops after four chimes and Mrs Carrington frowns

Lord Gilbert That can't be right, can it?
Dr Wilson I have seven o'clock, exactly.
Patterson Me too.
Miss Reid Don't break the circle, gentlemen.

They all join hands again

Mrs Carrington Is there anybody there?

Squeakily, the door opens R, *then slams shut with a terrific bang. Everybody
jumps, even Mrs Carrington, who quickly recovers her composure. Lady
Gilbert hugs herself*

Lady Gilbert It's suddenly very chilly in here.
Lord Gilbert Shall I fetch your wrap, my dear?

Lady Gilbert rejoins hands, reassuring her husband

Lady Gilbert No, no. It will pass. Something is happening now. Can't you
   feel it?

We hear footsteps across the floor and the side table is rocked

Mrs Carrington Why, it's Sergeant Major O'Connell, an old friend I haven't seen for a long time.
Miss Reid (*whispering*) Where is Chief Red Cloud?
Patterson Ssshh!
Mrs Carrington (*conducting a one-sided dialogue with the Sergeant Major*) I see. Yes, I quite understand. Red Cloud has been summoned to the death-bed of his grandson. The Sergeant Major will intercede for us tonight.
Lord Gilbert How sad. Send our condolences, Mrs Carrington.
Mrs Carrington (*conducting her conversation with the spirit*) Yes... Yes... I will. He says that there is one here to speak to Elizabeth. She is talking to me now...
Lord Gilbert Who could it be?
Mrs Carrington I sense a woman's presence. Why, Miss Reid, I do believe it is your mother. She says that she isn't sure about the colour, whatever that means.
Miss Reid Oh my. She must mean the house. I'm having it painted.
Mrs Carrington Pink! Pink, everywhere. Dazzling ... unbroken... Pink!
Miss Reid She doesn't like it. I knew she wouldn't like it. But, it's my house now and I can paint it any colour I want!
Patterson Calm yourself, Elizabeth.
Mrs Carrington I can see her now. She is wearing the same sober grey dress she always favoured and the cameo brooch you gave her.
Miss Reid Oh Mother, dear. Is she well?
Mrs Carrington All signs of her long sickness have gone. She is quite radiant. But there is something she must tell you... Yes, dear... I understand... She says that the charm bracelet you lost is to be found under the rug in your dressing room.
Miss Reid But ... that is precisely where the maid found it only this morning.
Lord Gilbert Remarkable!
Mrs Carrington And who is this hovering over your mother's shoulder? A tiny yellow bird. Wait. She is holding up her hand——
Miss Reid (*recoiling*) No, Mother, please! I can explain.
Mrs Carrington —as a warning. She says she has observed other changes in your life. A new friend.

Miss Reid and Patterson exchange a look

Miss Reid What of this new friend?
Mrs Carrington She is fading. I can barely see her. What? Fig and thistle? Whig and pistle? I can't be sure.

Miss Reid Whig and pistle? What can it mean, Edward?

Patterson I have no idea.

Dr Wilson Might it have been something else? There is a pub nearby called the *Pig and Whistle*.

Patterson chokes

Mrs Carrington I couldn't say. She was fading and the message was very faint. Sometimes the spirits are not as accommodating as we would like them to be.

Lord Gilbert Captain Patterson.

Patterson Yes, what?

Lord Gilbert You look quite flushed. Are you feeling all right?

Patterson A little hot, that's all.

Lady Gilbert Hot? But it's freezing in here.

Mrs Carrington Would you like some water, Captain Patterson?

Patterson No, I'll be fine. Please don't worry about it.

Mrs Carrington As you wish. (*She draws breath*) Ah, yes. There is another here to speak. To you, Lady Gilbert. Your aunt, I believe.

Lady Gilbert Dear Aunt…

Mrs Carrington She says she enjoyed the music on Saturday, but was sorry you had to leave so hurriedly.

Lady Gilbert The Vivaldi. It always brings on one of my heads.

Lord Gilbert Her ladyship's a martyr to her migraine attacks. She is often beset by them for days in a delirious condition, uttering all kinds of strange nonsense. And then, one morning she will awaken, quite exhausted, but herself once more.

Lady Gilbert With no remembrance of anything I have said or done.

Mrs Carrington Your aunt expresses certain reservations about a hat you purchased on … was it Monday?

Lady Gilbert My word, yes. The hat! What on earth could I have been thinking of? It has a dead animal in the brim.

Mrs Carrington A bird, according to your aunt.

Lady Gilbert I believe you're right. (*She laughs*) Yet, I cannot remember buying it.

Dr Wilson That's very curious. And you say this occurs frequently?

Lord Gilbert Not as often as it used to, John. We've become quite used to her "episodes".

Lady Gilbert smiles weakly, closes her eyes and softly rubs the area above her right eye with two fingers

Dr Wilson And yet, I do seem to remember, as a child, how you walked in your sleep one night all the way into the village, wearing nothing but your night-dress. The entire household, servants and all, followed you in a procession, too afraid to wake you up because we all thought that the shock might kill you.

Lord Gilbert I have told that story many times, but my wife has no recollection of the event.

Dr Wilson Cynthia. Cynthia; is something the matter?

Lady Gilbert sighs suddenly and faints, collapsing against her husband

Patterson Lady Gilbert? Are you all right?

Dr Wilson rises, goes to Lady Gilbert and kneels beside her

Lord Gilbert I thought this might happen. She fainted outside, you know. All the signs are there.

Patterson One of her episodes, you mean?

Lord Gilbert She's been very uneasy about coming here ever since these damned murders started happening.

Dr Wilson Her pulse is strong. Racing.

Mrs Carrington Do you have any salts, Doctor?

Dr Wilson Never without them. (*He produces a small vial from inside his coat, uncaps it and waves it under Lady Gilbert's nose*)

Lady Gilbert begins to recover as if from a bad dream

Miss Reid I can't say I blame her. We are right on his doorstep, after all.

Lady Gilbert He is here … he is here…

The rocking chair is suddenly hurled by an invisible force across the room. They all react with shock

Mrs Carrington What is happening? What was that noise?

Lady Gilbert starts to come around, crying out deliriously

Lady Gilbert He is here … he is here…

Patterson What's that? Who is here?

Dr Wilson We need some light in here. Captain Patterson, could you possibly…

Patterson Of course. (*He goes to the lamp switch and turns up the lights*)

Miss Reid Is she all right? Edward, I'm frightened.

Patterson goes to Miss Reid, comforts her

Dr Wilson (*to Mrs Carrington*) There is something very strange going on
    here, madam. (*He goes to the drinks tray and pours water into a glass for
    Lady Gilbert*)
Lord Gilbert There now, Cynthia. Back among the living, old girl.
Lady Gilbert Oh Bernard! Thank the Lord.
Lord Gilbert It's just another one of your turns, my dear.
Lady Gilbert No. No, it wasn't. This one was different.
Miss Reid What do you mean. How was it different?

Dr Wilson hands her the glass

Lady Gilbert (*haltingly*) I'm not sure. It was like a dream. I was in a dark
    place. There was someone else there and then there was pain. A terrible
    pain in my eyes. (*She drinks*)
Dr Wilson Fascinating.
Patterson I want no more of this. (*To Mrs Carrington*) You've gone too far
    with your parlour tricks, this time. Don't think I haven't seen through you
    from the start.
Lord Gilbert That's quite enough from you, young man.
Mrs Carrington No. I'm terribly sorry, but nothing like this has ever
    happened before.
Miss Reid Perhaps we shouldn't continue. You'd better ring for the maid,
    Edward.

Patterson goes to the bell pull

Patterson (*tugging the bell pull*) I'll take you home, Elizabeth. I knew this
    was a mistake.
Mrs Carrington That's strange.
Lord Gilbert What is?
Mrs Carrington I didn't hear anything.
Dr Wilson Why should you?
Mrs Carrington I have extremely acute hearing, Doctor. I can always hear
    Mary's bell, even from this room.
Dr Wilson Try again, Patterson.

Patterson pulls again

Anything?
Mrs Carrington No.

Patterson It's probably broken. I'll fetch the girl myself. (*He tries the door*) It's locked.
Mrs Carrington Impossible. There is no lock on that door.
Patterson (*trying it*) Jammed then. Either way, I can't open it.
Lord Gilbert Let me try, then. (*He tries*) It won't budge.
Patterson (*banging on it*) Mary. Open up, for goodness sake.
Miss Reid Whatever's happened to the girl?
Mrs Carrington I have no idea. But, wait a minute, listen.

They are all quiet

Miss Reid (*whispering*) What are we listening for?
Patterson I can hear nothing.
Dr Wilson (*to Mrs Carrington*) What can *you* hear?
Mrs Carrington Nothing.
Patterson Wonderful! She can hear nothing, because there is nothing to hear.
Mrs Carrington But that's what is so strange. The street outside is usually quite busy, even at this hour. Yet, I hear no hansom cabs, no pedlars, and even my old clock…
Dr Wilson It's stopped. Right on the hour.
Lord Gilbert (*producing his watch*) Well, I can tell you the time, if that's what you want. That's strange. It's not working.

All the men examine their watches and tap them

Dr Wilson What the deuce…?
Patterson Mine has stopped too. What's going on here?
Mrs Carrington I'm not sure.
Patterson Oh, come on, don't play the innocent. You've surpassed yourself this time, but enough is enough. I don't know how you did it, but I think it's time you gave us an explanation.
Mrs Carrington (*emphatically*) I'm telling you, I have no idea!

They are all taken aback by the force of her response

Lady Gilbert (*quietly*) It's almost as if time is standing still.

They all consider this for a loaded moment

Miss Reid (*to Lady Gilbert*) You said something before.
Lady Gilbert Did I?

Miss Reid When you fainted. You said something.
Lady Gilbert My eyes. The terrible pain.
Miss Reid No. You said "He is here".
Lord Gilbert Who is here?

They all look at Lady Gilbert

Lady Gilbert I don't remember saying it.
Patterson I heard you say it too.
Dr Wilson We all heard you say it.
Lady Gilbert (*shaking her head*) It wasn't me.
Patterson Of course it was you. How can you possibly deny it?
Lord Gilbert Captain Patterson, will you please stop brow-beating my wife.
    Can't you see what has plainly occurred, any of you?

They are all quiet, uncomprehending

    Cynthia has been possessed by a soul in torment. It's as plain as day.
Patterson I need a brandy! (*He pours himself a drink*)
Lord Gilbert It was bound to happen. For months now we have opened our
    minds to the other side, inviting them to cross over. We all assumed that
    Mrs Carrington was the preferred medium for any spirit entity. But it
    would appear that in this instance my wife is the most suitable host.
Patterson And you're saying we have an uninvited guest.
Lord Gilbert Precisely.
Miss Reid But who?
Lord Gilbert Perhaps Mrs Carrington could tell us that.
Mrs Carrington I'm afraid I can't. Nothing quite like this has ever happened
    before.
Patterson I thought as much.
Lord Gilbert Your flippancy is beginning to get on my nerves, young man.
Mrs Carrington Of course. There is one way we could find out.

They all look meaningfully at Lady Gilbert

Dr Wilson Out of the question. Cynthia has had one terrible shock tonight.
    I don't know if she can take another.
Lady Gilbert Thank you for your concern, John, but I think I can make that
    decision for myself.
Miss Reid You mean you will do it?
Mrs Carrington If we are ever to leave this room, I believe I must. Quickly
    now, before I lose courage.

All hold hands, like before. Patterson sighs

Miss Reid You too, Edward.

Patterson sulks

Please.
Patterson This is pointless. Oh, all right.
Mrs Carrington Everybody, close your eyes and whatever happens try to
stay calm. Is there anybody there? Is there anybody there?

After a few deep breaths, the Lights go dim and Lady Gilbert moans

Lord Gilbert Cynthia?
Lady Gilbert (*with a Cockney accent*) It's dark. Why is it so very dark?
Miss Reid Lady Gilbert? Is that you?
Mrs Carrington I don't think so.
Lord Gilbert Then who is it?

On the mirror behind them, the letters "IVY" appear, scrawled in blood

Miss Reid Oh, my God. Look at that!
Dr Wilson Not so loud, Miss Reid. You'll break her trance.
Lord Gilbert Ivy?
Patterson Ivy? It can't be.

They all look at Patterson suspiciously

Lady Gilbert Who is there? Please answer me.
Lord Gilbert You're among friends, dear, don't fret.
Lady Gilbert (*coyly*) I know there is somebody there. You've been
following me. Show yourself now. Don't be shy.
Mrs Carrington She isn't talking to us. Oh dear. I don't like the sound of
this.
Lady Gilbert Now you're being silly. Come on. I won't bite. Leastways, not
unless you want me to.
Miss Reid Whatever does she mean?

Patterson shrugs

Lady Gilbert All right, then. Hide yourself, see if I care. But it's a cold night
to be outside on your own. I've got a lovely little room nearby. Real toasty
it is. If you bought us a bottle of gin…

Dr Wilson It's last night. The name of the prostitute who was killed on her way home was Ivy Potter.

Patterson The murderer must have been following her from the pub.

Miss Reid From the pub, Edward. How would you know that?

Patterson (*stammering*) I just assumed——

Lady Gilbert Sod you then! Lurkin' about in the dark and frightening decent folk. I'll get the peelers on to you, see if I don't.

Lord Gilbert If this is going where I think it's going…

Lady Gilbert Evenin' Billy! You goin' my way, love, I could do with a bit of light. Never mind then. I'll just have to feel my way, eh darlin'. Oh, you cheeky bugger! (*She laughs and starts to hum a Victorian music hall tune*)

Mrs Carrington Billy?

Dr Wilson The last person to see Ivy Potter alive was one William Spandler, lamp lighter by trade, known throughout the district as Billy the Spark. He was midway through his shift when they had that very conversation.

Miss Reid Did he see anybody else?

Dr Wilson Moments later. A dark, hooded figure, moving very lightly, passed him by in the same direction Ivy took.

Lady Gilbert Billy? Is that you? (*She listens for a few seconds*) It's you again, isn't it? My secret admirer. I'm warnin' you, I've got a hat pin here, and I know how to use it on a shady cove like you, so watch it, or I'll stick yer.

Dr Wilson An empty threat, but she was beginning to get frightened.

Miss Reid I'm beginning to get frightened.

Mrs Carrington We mustn't let this go too far. We can break the circle by simply letting go, but even that has its dangers.

Patterson The shock of it…

Mrs Carrington Yes.

Lady Gilbert He's still there, in the shadows behind me. I can hear him sliding along the wall of the alley, where it's darkest. Damn these shoes, how they pinch! I can hardly walk. I know a place, up ahead. It's dark. Safe. Oh God! What if it's him? What if it's him who did those two girls. I won't run. I mustn't. He'll catch me for sure, hobbled like this.

Mrs Carrington Oh, the poor child, I can hardly bear it.

Lady Gilbert He's getting closer. These bloody shoes. I've got to take 'em off, it'll only take a second. Gawd, that's better. Bleedin' cold, though.

Dr Wilson Now, you *do* have me.

Lord Gilbert What?

Dr Wilson The shoes. She couldn't possibly have known that.

Lady Gilbert He's running. Not far now. If I get a move on, I can hide and watch the bastard pass by.

Miss Reid Perhaps she saw him. Perhaps she knows who he is.

Lady Gilbert There it is. Mrs Parker's Pie Shop. I can hide in the doorway, it's dark and deep.

Dr Wilson The police found her shoes beside the body. It was one of the details they didn't release to the press.

Patterson One of the details?

Mrs Carrington Quiet. I think it's about to happen.

Miss Reid We can't allow it.

Lady Gilbert (*breathing heavily*) Blimey, my heart is beatin' fit to burst. I can hear him getting closer. Oh Lord, there he goes, past the doorway off down the alley. Gawd, what a relief. (*She gasps*) Oh no! I dropped the shoes … he's stopped … he's coming back!

Miss Reid We musn't continue. None of us know what might happen to her ladyship if we allow the murder to run its course.

Dr Wilson A moment longer. If she only gets a look at his face.

Lady Gilbert He's here. He's here! (*She becomes desperately frightened—repeating it over and over on a rising crescendo until she raises her hands to her eyes and screams*)

Blood pours down from behind her hands and confusion ensues

Lord Gilbert My God, Cynthia, wake up!

Miss Reid She's bleeding!

Mrs Carrington Doctor. What's happening?

Lady Gilbert collapses in her husband's arms

Dr Wilson I don't know. She's fainted again. Yes, there's a pulse. Quite strong.

Patterson Where did all that blood come from?

Dr Wilson Her eyes, I think. Help me get her to the couch.

They take her to the couch

Miss Reid (*panicky*) I told you we should stop, didn't I? I told you.

Patterson All right, Elizabeth, calm down.

Lord Gilbert Is she going to be all right, John?

Dr Wilson I can't say. (*He wipes her bloody face*) That's strange. There don't appear to be any wounds.

Miss Reid But the blood…

Patterson She must have scratched herself with her own nails.

Dr Wilson No. I can see no cuts on the eyes or the skin around them. It's almost as if…

Mrs Carrington Almost as if what?

Dr Wilson Well. I have heard of similar things happening. Usually to religious zealots at moments of divine revelation but, I suppose, under these conditions, it might be possible.

Mrs Carrington Stigmata, Doctor?

Dr Wilson Yes. You know of such things, of course.

Patterson Stig… what?

Dr Wilson Stigmata. Wounds which occur spontaneously in certain Christian mystics and correspond to those inflicted on Our Lord at the crucifixion.

Mrs Carrington Such people usually bleed from the hands or feet. Sometimes from the abdomen where a spear was thrust, or from the head where the crown of thorns was placed.

Patterson But from the eyes?

Dr Wilson An hysterical reaction perhaps. I don't know. Let's try the smelling salts, again. (*He wafts them under her nose*)

Lady Gilbert coughs and wakes, crying out and flailing

It's all right. You're among friends now.

Lady Gilbert (*collapsing back on to the couch with a sigh of relief*) Oh! That poor, wretched girl.

Lord Gilbert Can you tell us what happened, dear?

Lady Gilbert It was terrible. There are no words…

Miss Reid Did you see him?

Lady Gilbert I saw nothing, nothing but shadows.

Miss Reid Your eyes were bleeding. Do they hurt?

Lady Gilbert Not any more. But when he had me… (*She buries her face in her hands, shaking her head*)

Patterson So, you didn't see his face or hear his voice?

Lady Gilbert No. I only felt his hands in Ivy's hair, seeking out her face, her eyes. And then his fingers, pushing in. Such strong hands.

Patterson (*to Miss Reid, who is holding his hand*) Elizabeth. You are hurting me.

Miss Reid (*releasing him*) I'm sorry.

Mrs Carrington My God, surely he didn't.

Dr Wilson I'm afraid he did. That was the other detail the police held back. The fact that all the victims' eyes were removed before their deaths.

Miss Reid Thank God we broke the link when we did.

Dr Wilson Yes, there was much worse to come.

Lord Gilbert Before their deaths, you say. Why? Why would he do that?

Dr Wilson We're not sure. It could be that he didn't want his victims to escape or identify him.

Mrs Carrington So, it might have been somebody she knew.

Dr Wilson Perhaps. Certainly it is somebody who is familiar with the area. He might even live nearby, although we can't be sure of it.

Miss Reid Edward?

Patterson My dear?

Miss Reid (*uncertainly*) I am sure you … reacted … when the name Ivy Potter was mentioned. Did you know this woman?

Patterson (*gabbling*) I … I … well … I mean…

Mrs Carrington He did know her. I can attest to that.

Patterson What do you mean? I've never even met the woman.

Mrs Carrington I think you have. At the *Pig and Whistle* on Thursday afternoons.

Patterson (*aghast*) How could you know that?

Miss Reid So it's true!

Patterson (*to Miss Reid after a moment's reflection*) Yes, it's true, dammit! (*To Mrs Carrington*) But how could you know that?

Dr Wilson Because she had you followed.

Patterson Followed?

Dr Wilson She had all of us followed. As soon as I saw Mary tonight, I recognized her. You really shouldn't use such pretty shadows, Mrs Carrington.

Mrs Carrington Is she so pretty?

Patterson Of course, it all makes sense now. Your "uncanny" insight into our lives.

Lady Gilbert Mrs Carrington!

Mrs Carrington It is so.

Patterson Such a bloody sham!

Lord Gilbert That's enough!

Patterson She's as good as admitted it. She's been leading us up the garden path from the start. God knows how we didn't fathom it out for ourselves.

Miss Reid We wanted to believe.

Lady Gilbert So, it's all been a lie then?

Mrs Carrington No. Not all. Not this evening.

Patterson It's a trick, isn't it. Something you and her ladyship have cooked up between you.

Dr Wilson I don't think so. Everything I have seen tonight tallies with facts which are known only to a chosen few.

Patterson Mrs Carrington is a resourceful woman. Maybe she has a friend in the police force. With Lady Gilbert here as her accomplice…

Mrs Carrington What would be the point? To expose myself, like this, as a charlatan?

Miss Reid (*to Lady Gilbert*) You said "He is here". And you knew her, Edward.

Patterson I knew her vaguely. Elizabeth, you have to understand. She meant nothing to me, it was just——

Miss Reid Was she blackmailing you, Edward? Did she threaten to expose you to me?

Patterson It was nothing like that.

Miss Reid All this time, Edward. I should have listened to my mother. She never trusted men.

Patterson Oh, Elizabeth! I didn't kill Ivy Potter.

Lord Gilbert And why should we believe you?

Patterson (*sighing*) Because I was with somebody else, that evening. You met her, Elizabeth, tonight, outside this very house.

Miss Reid But … you said… Oh!

Lord Gilbert It's plain to all of us, young man, that you are a practised liar. If the killer is in this room, it is likely to be the man who knew the victim. You might have known them all, for all we know.

Patterson And so might you!

Lord Gilbert How dare you!

Miss Reid Stop it, Edward!

Patterson It's true though. Didn't your wife tell us that on Thursday nights you attend your club?

Lady Gilbert For as long as we have been married.

Miss Reid Thursday nights. The killer always strikes on a Thursday.

Dr Wilson Mrs Carrington. Did you ever bother to have Lord Gilbert followed on Thursday nights?

Mrs Carrington Only once. But that was before the murders started.

Lord Gilbert This is preposterous!

Patterson Well, now you know how it feels. Welcome to the club.

Dr Wilson Let's stop fighting amongst ourselves for a moment. There is some purpose for all of this and we are overlooking a vital point.

A pause

Mrs Carrington Please continue, Doctor. What is this vital point?

Dr Wilson We are all assuming that the killer is a man.

Miss Reid *He* is here. That's what Ivy said.

Dr Wilson Yes, but she would have made the same assumption as we did. We all heard her last moments. She was in the dark, then blinded. How do we know her attacker wasn't a woman?

Miss Reid Women don't do such things.

Dr Wilson (*shaking his head and laughing ironically*) In some cultures, the women are more feared for their cruelty than the men. They are capable, believe me.

Lady Gilbert Are you trying to say that one of us ladies might be the killer, John?

Dr Wilson What I'm saying, Cynthia, is that, with the obvious exception of Mrs Carrington, any one of us might be.

Patterson I'll go along with that. No blind woman could do this thing. Not even one as devious as Mrs Carrington.

Lord Gilbert Careful, Patterson, you are still our leading suspect.

Patterson Think what you like. I know I am innocent, even if I can't prove it. None of us can.

Lady Gilbert Even me? What possible reason could I have for slaying these young women?

Patterson I can't say why, but you certainly had the opportunity. On Thursday evenings you were alone in the house after your husband left for his club. And the details you have revealed tonight—why, even the eminent Dr Wilson has attested to the fact that they could only have been known by a privileged few. Including the murderer.

Lord Gilbert You go too far, young man.

Patterson I've barely started. And what of our good doctor, here? Isn't it strange that these murders began only a few weeks after he arrived in the area?

Mrs Carrington But the doctor is helping the police with their inquiries.

Patterson Because of the very nature of the deaths, madam. The eyes were gouged from their skulls. Isn't it possible that there was another reason for this apparent mutilation?

Dr Wilson What are you talking about?

Patterson Research, Doctor. You can't legitimately take the eyes of the living; and the eyes of the dead are too cold or atrophied. You need fresh meat!

Lord Gilbert Don't listen to him, John.

Miss Reid Why not accuse me as well, Edward. I had good reason to kill Ivy Potter, had I but known what she was to you.

Patterson Elizabeth. I know I have behaved abominably, but you must believe me. I am not a murderer.

Miss Reid I just don't know.

Patterson (*going to the door*) None of us will know anything until we get out of this blessed room!

Mrs Carrington We won't get out until we have an answer. And that answer is here. That's what Ivy is trying to tell us.

Lord Gilbert Let's think calmly about this for a moment.

Miss Reid Something did occur to me, although I'm not sure you won't think it's foolish.

Mrs Carrington Go on, my dear.

Miss Reid It's about the eyes, really. Isn't there some silly superstition about how the eyes of a murder victim record the image of their attacker, even after their death?

Dr Wilson As you say: a silly superstition. There is no scientific evidence that such things occur.

Lord Gilbert You know that, and now so do we. But does the murderer? If he believes the eyes will betray him, then that might explain why he takes them.

Lady Gilbert Perhaps there is more to it than that. What if there is another reason for him not to be seen?

Patterson What else can there be?

Lady Gilbert Shame, perhaps? He knows that what he is doing is terribly wrong and evil. He can't abide to be seen by his victims.

Mrs Carrington (*shocked*) What?

Dr Wilson Is there something wrong, Mrs Carrington?

Mrs Carrington No, but Lady Gilbert. You just said something … it reminded me.

Dr Wilson She said "He cannot abide to be seen".

Mrs Carrington But that's almost what Mary said…

Lady Gilbert Mary? What do you mean?

Mrs Carrington (*to Lady Gilbert*) And you said "He is here"… Oh, my God! He is here!

The clock strikes three more times

Mary enters with a tray of tea things

Lord Gilbert Mary. Where on earth have you been?

Mary Making the tea, sir. It only took a minute.

Patterson But that's not possible, is it?

Dr Wilson checks his watch

Dr Wilson My watch. It's started again.

Lord Gilbert Mine also.

Patterson But why?

A knocking on the floor

Lady Gilbert What's that knocking?

Lord Gilbert It's coming from down there.

Mary Dodgy plumbing. It's always done that.

Patterson The door. My God, we can leave.

Mary Sir? You've only just arrived.
Mrs Carrington Mary, give me your arm and let us all leave immediately.
Dr Wilson Allow me. Hold that door open, Bernard.

All except Mary and Miss Reid exit

Miss Reid There's somebody down there. Listen. Edward?
Mary He's gone, ma'am.

Miss Reid leaves hastily

Shall I bring the tea, ma'am?

Mary exits, leaving the door open

The knocking continues. The Lights dim. The rug concealing the trapdoor is thrown back by invisible hands. The door is thrown open and a shaft of dim light from below lights the empty room. Silence

Hopkins comes up, looking around

Hopkins I'm awfully sorry, ma'am, but I can't seem to make the machinery work. (*His words fade off*) Hello?

The door slams by invisible hands. He crosses to it. It is jammed again

Is there anybody there?

Behind him the trap door slams. He turns, startled. Alone in the darkness of the room, he nervously speaks

Is there anybody there?

The face of the murdered woman appears in the mirror above the mantle, lit eerily from below

Hopkins slumps to his knees in submission as the Lights slowly fade down

CURTAIN

PRODUCTION NOTES

In the absence of a trapdoor I suggest a cupboard on stage with fake apparatus inside to suggest a box of tricks. It is important that Hopkins does not actually leave the room but is an invisible presence in it which the spirits can sense, but which the living cannot.

The effect of Lady Gilbert "bleeding from the eyes" was achieved in the first production by having small sacs of blood concealed on the set (perhaps under the table). The actress palmed them, then pressed them against her eyes to squeeze the blood out.

The mirror was plain glass on a flat. About a foot behind it was draped a black-out curtain. A stage hand wearing black clothes and gloves painted "IVY" on the inside of the glass with red emulsion paint.

A light over the mirror came on to reveal the face of Ivy at the right moment. She wore a black scarf over her head and the light came up slowly as she turned to reveal her face.

Lee Flewitt

FURNITURE AND PROPERTY LIST

Further dressing may be added at the director's discretion

On stage: Table. *On it*: crystal ball. *Under its top*: sacs of blood
6 chairs
Side table. *On it*: drinks tray with pitcher of water, bottle of brandy, glasses
Couch
Rocking chair
Bookshelves holding books and vase
Gas lamps
Clock
Mirror
Rug covering trap door
Bell pull
White cane

Off stage: Tray of tea things (**Mary**)

Personal: **Mary**: apron, notebook
Dr Wilson: small vial
All Men: watches

LIGHTING PLOT

Property fittings required: gas lamps. Practical fittings required: crystal ball
Interior. The same throughout

To open: Crystal ball glows, gas lamps on with covering lights

Cue 1   **Mrs Carrington**: "Is there anybody there?"   (Page 1)
Crystal ball flickers slightly; gas lamps flicker

Cue 2   **Mrs Carrington**: "…little skivvy for that chore."   (Page 2)
Bring lights up

Cue 3   **Lord Gilbert** turns down the gas lamps   (Page 14)
Fade gas lamps and covering lights down

Cue 4   **Patterson** turns up the lights   (Page 18)
Fade lights up

Cue 5   **Mrs Carrington** takes a few deep breaths   (Page 21)
Fade lights down

Cue 6   **Mary** exits and knocking continues   (Page 29)
Dim lights

Cue 7   Trapdoor is thrown open   (Page 29)
Snap on shaft of dim light from below

Cue 8   **Hopkins**: "Is there anybody there?"   (Page 29)
*Slowly bring up light on **Ivy**'s face from below*

Cue 9   **Hopkins** slumps to his knees   (Page 29)
Slowly fade lights down

EFFECTS PLOT

Cue 1	To open *Clock ticks loudly, then chimes thirteen times*	(Page 1)
Cue 2	**Mrs Carrington**: "Enter, spirit, you are among friends." *Door slowly opens and closes on squeaky hinges.* *Footsteps cross room*	(Page 1)
Cue 3	**Mrs Carrington**: "…let us know your name." *Rocking chair starts to rock*	(Page 1)

Cue 4	**Mrs Carrington**: "It must find expression!"
	Books fly off bookshelves, picture is dislodged from wall,
	    vase breaks and general havoc ensues with storm of
	    sound effects. Table rises from floor, hovering
		(Page 2)

Cue 5	**Mrs Carrington**: "Spirits, cease!" *Cut effects, but table continues to hover*	(Page 2)
Cue 6	**Mrs Carrington**: "Spirits cease, Mr Hopkins!" *Table drops with a clatter*	(Page 2)
Cue 7	**Mrs Carrington** sits and picks up a book *Clock ticks for about fifteen seconds, then sound of* *knocking at front door*	(Page 9)
Cue 8	**Dr Wilson**: "…usually get to the truth of them." *Knocking and more voices off*	(Page 11)
Cue 9	**Mrs Carrington**: "It's not entirely up to me." *Clock chimes four times*	(Page 14)
Cue 10	**Mrs Carrington**: "Is there anybody there?" *Door squeakily opens, then slams shut with terrific bang*	(Page 14)
Cue 11	**Lady Gilbert**: "Can't you feel it?" *Footsteps across floor; side table is rocked*	(Page 15)